The Harrier
Story

Also in this series:

. . . and coming soon
The Hurricane Story

The Harrier Story

Peter R. March

Sutton Publishing

Sutton Publishing Limited
Phoenix Mill, Thrupp, Stroud
Gloucestershire, GL5 2BU

First published 2007

British Library Cataloguing in Publication Data
A catalogue for this book is available from the British Library.

ISBN 978-0-7509-4487-8

Typeset in 9.5/14.5pt Syntax.
Typesetting and origination by
Sutton Publishing Limited.
Printed and bound in England by
J.H. Haynes & Co. Ltd, Sparkford.

➤
*Harrier family – top to
bottom, GR3/T4/FRS1/
GR5 and GR7.*

CONTENTS

The story of the Harrier's emergence from the drawing boards of the Bristol Aeroplane Company's Engine Division and Hawker Aircraft nearly fifty years ago, through to today's highly successful product from British Aerospace, McDonnell Douglas and Rolls-Royce, is long and complex. I am grateful to the authors of the many published references that have been used to compile this short narrative, and in particular Roy Braybrook's *Harrier – The Vertical Reality* published by Royal Air Force Benevolent Fund Enterprises in 1996.

I am indebted to some of the 'pioneers' of V/STOL flight, who have allowed me to quote from their well-documented trials and tribulations, and Harrier test pilots Bill Bedford, John Farley and Duncan Simpson, who have provided colour to the 'story'. I would particularly like to thank Brian Strickland, who has carefully researched and collated information and photographs.

With a wealth of images available to illustrate *The Harrier Story* it has been difficult to narrow the choice down. I would like to thank Patrick Allen, Gordon Bartley, Derek Bower, Phil Boyden, Richard Butcher, Leslie Custalov, Neil Dunridge, Ted Herman, Jamie Hunter, John Hutchinson, Geoff Lee, Andrew March, Daniel March, Robbie Robinson, Mike Stroud, and the former photographers at Hawker Siddeley Aviation and British Aerospace at Dunsfold and Warton, Bristol Siddeley Engines and Rolls-Royce at Filton, and the McDonnell Douglas Corporation in the USA, for the excellent photographs that I have been able to draw upon.

Photographs: Peter R. March/PRM Aviation Collection, unless otherwise credited.

In a press release dated 25 November 1960, Hawker Aircraft confirmed the existence of a revolutionary new military aircraft that promised to combine the unique take-off and landing ability of the helicopter with the conventional performance of a jet fighter.

The resulting P.1127/Harrier family of vertical/short take-off and landing (V/STOL) combat aircraft, and the Rolls-Royce Pegasus series of vectored-thrust turbofans, together formed one of Britain's most important contributions to postwar military aviation technology. Rather than using rotors or direct jet thrust, the P.1127 had an innovative vectored-thrust turbofan engine. It should also be remembered that the original powerplant concept was a derivative of a French invention, and that the aircraft would never have seen the light of day without substantial American support. The Harrier/Pegasus combination ultimately proved to be a very successful international product.

Back more than half a century, the very fact that the P.1127's empty weight would decide whether or not the new aircraft could leave the ground by jet-lift alone, raised considerable doubt in people's minds about the project. Hawker Aircraft had built its reputation on single-engined fighters, largely powered by Rolls-Royce engines, that looked superb and were highly

'Everything we put up is rejected by either the RAF or Royal Navy – and sometimes both.'

Sir Sydney Camm, when designing the ill-fated P.1154, which was cancelled on 2 February 1965

Did you know?
In the early 1960s a former Chief of the Air Staff said: 'The Press ought to be told that such a machine is a toy, and quite useless for operational reasons.'

The P.1127 was clearly not going to be a Hunter replacement over a wide range of combat roles. Its marketability was completely unknown and unpredictable, although it was clear from the outset that installing twice the thrust of a conventional ground attack aircraft would not make for a low-cost aircraft. Developing the Harrier family represented a significant break for Hawker away from multi-role conventional fighters.

More than forty years later, the Harrier, albeit in significantly different versions, is still very much in active service with the Royal Air Force, the US Marine Corps and the navies of India, Spain and Thailand. Produced by the successor companies – Hawker Siddeley, British Aircraft Corporation, British Aerospace and BAE Systems in the UK and McDonnell Douglas (now part

manoeuvrable, but were by no means lightweight. The ultimate Hawker fighter was the solid and reliable Hunter, powered by a Rolls-Royce Avon turbojet, which had a good performance and a long-lasting airframe, and sold in large numbers.

of the Boeing empire) in the USA, the Harrier has proved its worth to Britain in the Falklands, Belize, Iraq, the Balkans and Afghanistan and to the US Marine Corps for carrier and land-based operations around the world, not least in the Middle East.

Through the first decade of the twenty-first century the British Aerospace/McDonnell Douglas Harrier family continues to be the world's only high-performance V/STOL combat aircraft to see service on a significant scale, just as its Rolls-Royce Pegasus vectored-thrust turbofan remains the only series-built V/STOL engine.

➤
Three of the six P.1127s flying together in 1962.

Although V/STOL had its true origins in Germany during the Second World War – the rocket-powered Bachem Ba 349 Natter (Adder) had made its first piloted flight in February 1945 – practical progress had to wait until the 1950s, when jet engines were far more advanced and there was a stronger operational motivation.

The successful development of jet engines was, by the 1950s, producing powerplants with a thrust that was very much greater. This offered the possibility of aircraft that could take off vertically, thereby not requiring long, expensive and vulnerable runways.

Rolls-Royce developed the Thrust Measuring Rig (TMR), popularly known as the 'Flying Bedstead' in 1953 to test this principle with two Nene turbojets, at that time one of the most powerful in the world.

◄◄
Harrier GR7 of No. 1 Squadron firing Matra 155 SNEB rockets.

▲
The Bachem Ba 349 Natter (Adder), a Second World War German rocket-powered aircraft that made its first pilotless vertical launch on 23 February 1945.

5

First airborne in 1954, the Rolls-Royce Thrust Measuring Rig was followed four years later by the Short SC.1 experimental vertical-take-off aircraft. (BSS Collection)

This was to discover whether jet-borne flight could be safely controlled by the pilot. A control system, devised in association with RAE Farnborough, used jet reaction from 'puffer jets' carried on long outriggers and fed with high-pressure air bled from the engine compressors.

Tests with the Flying Bedstead, culminated in its first untethered flight on 3 August 1954, piloted by R.T. Shepherd. This showed that pilots could achieve stable hovering flight and paved the way for the development of the control system still used today on the Harrier. The machine is now

A tilting platform for vertical-attitude take-off and landing was used by the Ryan X-13 Vertijet.

The Bell X-14A featured a nose-mounted jet engine for its thrust-vectoring. (BSS Collection)

preserved in the Science Museum, South Kensington.

One of the driving forces behind V/STOL development came from the USA, where the US Navy funded the Lockheed XFV-1 and Convair XFY-1 turboprop 'tail-sitters', but these tests ceased in 1956. A third US tailsitter was the single-seat Ryan X-13 Vertijet. Powered by a 10,000lb (44.5kN) Rolls-Royce Avon turbojet it became the world's first jet-powered VTOL research aircraft when it was flown on 10 December 1955. It featured a hook mounted beneath the forward fuselage from which it was suspended for take-off, and was launched from and recovered to a tilting platform. But the tailsitter was very limited, and attention increasingly turned to the flat-riser, which required less mental gymnastics from the pilot.

With a high-set delta-wing, the X-13 had no landing gear and was designed to take off vertically. Two prototypes were built and the first complete transition from vertical take-off to horizontal flight – and a vertical landing – was accomplished on 11 April 1957. The Vertijet proved to be successful and was at one time thought likely to form the basis for the projected XF-109 VTOL fighter for the USAF.

What made possible a comparatively simple V/STOL combat aircraft was the invention of a new type of powerplant. The thrust from this new engine could be turned through more than 90°, rotating about a point very close to the engine's centre of gravity. This vectored-thrust engine was fitted to the Bell X-14, which made its first conventional flight and hovers in 1957, and achieved the transition from horizontal to vertical flight on 24 May 1958. This is regarded as the world's first successful vectored-thrust V/STOL demonstrator.

Did you know?
In 1964, the USAF stuck to the view that V/STOL was not worthwhile, and still expected the General Dynamics F-111 to sell all over the world as the next-generation all-can-do military aircraft. This view held back development of V/STOL combat aircraft.

The need for a combat aircraft that could be dispersed away from main bases arose in the early days of the Cold War, as Western fears grew that the Soviet Union would soon possess literally thousands of tactical nuclear weapons, which could be delivered accurately against large, fixed targets by manned aircraft and ballistic missiles.

It quickly became apparent that V/STOL aircraft would be extremely expensive (perhaps twice the cost of conventional designs), and that there would be significant problems in operating them from dispersed sites.

Their complexity implied serious difficulties in maintaining a high standard of availability at dispersal. Their high-energy jets made operation from grass airfields unlikely on a year-round basis. There were also worries concerning site security, dependable communications between the sites and their control centres, and the storage of nuclear weapons at small, dispersed sites. It took several years for the RAF to accept that the Harrier really did provide unique survivability when operating from dispersed sites in West Germany.

V/STOL required a type of powerplant that would in effect provide extra lift with little weight increase – in other words a system of much higher than normal thrust/weight ratio. There were two basic ways to achieve a large amount of jet lift without excessive weight. One was to link the propulsion engine to some innovative device that would magnify its thrust by allowing it to deal with a much larger mass flow of air. A helicopter-type rotor was ruled out by a fighter's dimensions, but this thrust

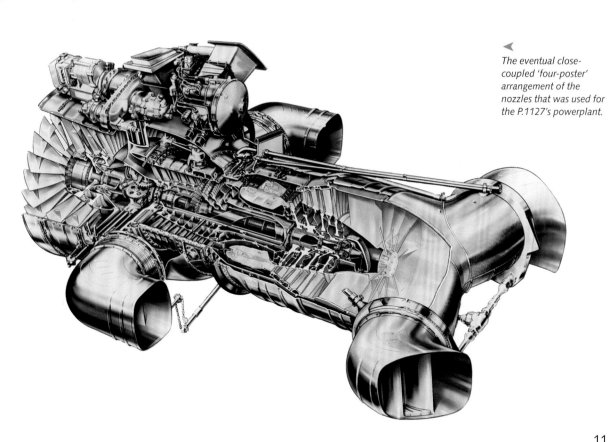

◄

The eventual close-coupled 'four-poster' arrangement of the nozzles that was used for the P.1127's powerplant.

magnification device could take the form of buried fans, called 'dedicated' lift engines.

At Patchway, near Bristol, it fell to Gordon Lewis at the Bristol Aeroplane Company's Engine Division, a young project engineer who later became a director of Rolls-Royce, to produce plans clearly presenting the advantages of thrust magnification, continuous jet-vectoring and an acceptable position for the powerplant centre of gravity. This eliminated the disadvantage of multiple gearboxes, and long drive-shafts to remote fans. He suggested a single axial-flow fan, mounted coaxial with the engine, and exhausting through a rotatable nozzle on either side of the fan casing. Aside from being far simpler, this concept allowed Bristol to use a fan that was already in development, in the form of the first two stages from the low-pressure compressor for its Olympus 21 engine.

The Bristol Orion was initially proposed but the Orpheus was subsequently chosen. This had as its compressor the low-speed spool from the Orion, thus giving similar power potential. A new two-stage power turbine was added to the Orpheus, designed to run at the same speed as the Olympus fan, which it would drive by means of a shaft turning inside that of the Orpheus. The outcome was a much lighter engine with a close-coupled 'four-poster' arrangement of the jets.

The P.1127, as proposed, was sufficiently promising to initiate a self-funded collaborative effort between Hawker Aircraft at Kingston and Bristol Engine Company at Patchway, Bristol, in the autumn of 1957, although at the time both companies had other more important projects on hand.

US Mutual Weapons Development Program representatives were shown a brochure at Farnborough in September 1957, and commented that twice as much flying radius would be required if the P.1127 was to have a useful military potential. A considerable increase in thrust was clearly necessary to achieve such an improvement in range. The Government had selected the Short SC.1 powered by Rolls-

Rolls-Royce provided RB-108 lift engines for the Short SC.1's V/STOL flight, along with a conventional propulsion engine.

Did you know?

While hovering or flying at very low speeds, the Harrier is controlled in roll, pitch and yaw by reaction control jets located in the wingtips, the nose and tail.

Royce RB.108 lift engines to provide V/STOL know-how – and said that no alternatives would be supported. If British Government policy had been imposed on Bristol and Hawker, there would have been no Pegasus engine and no Harrier.

By March 1958, the design of the Hawker P.1127 was broadly similar to the form of the prototype that was to commence hovering trials about thirty months later. The centre fuselage was filled by the relatively large diameter of the engine, which was to receive its air through two intakes that were extremely short (roughly equal in length to one engine diameter) and of semicircular cross-section.

The pilot was accommodated in a rather cramped cockpit, which was not raised to give a rear view. Early attempts to have two main undercarriage units mounted in the fuselage sides just ahead of the rear nozzles were abandoned because of possible blast damage to the tyres. They were replaced by a single main unit mounted just behind the engine, resulting in what was termed for marketing purposes a 'zero-track tricycle' configuration. The P.1127 undercarriage load distribution was somewhat

'We believe that there is an urgent need for an operational version of the P.1127. As soon as it can be negotiated, a contract will be placed for a limited development programme so that the RAF can have, by the time they need it, an aircraft that will in fact be the first in the field, with vertical take-off for close-support of our land forces.'

Prime Minister Harold Wilson on 2 February 1965

between that of a 'bicycle' and a 'tricycle' arrangement: the nose unit of the Harrier GR1 typically supported 38 per cent of the aircraft weight. There were 'outrigger' wheels at the wingtips to provide lateral balance on the ground.

The angular position of the four engine nozzles was to be selected by a single lever, mounted just inboard of the quadrant on the left-hand console. The lever controlled the supply of high-pressure air to two motors, mounted under the engine. These

The unmarked first P.1127 prototype had its first tethered hop at Dunsfold airfield on 21 October 1960.

Did you know?

The Harrier has two control elements that a normal fighter aircraft does not usually have. These are the thrust vector and reaction control. The thrust vector is the slant of the four engine nozzles and can be set between 0° (horizontal, pointing directly backwards) and 98° (pointing slightly forwards). Thrust vector is adjusted by a control close to and next to the thrust lever. The reaction control is achieved by manipulating the control stick and is similar in action to the cyclic control of a helicopter.

Third development P.1127 (XP980) had a more powerful (14,000lb st) Pegasus 3 engine.

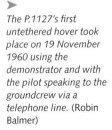

The P.1127's first untethered hover took place on 19 November 1960 using the demonstrator and with the pilot speaking to the groundcrew via a telephone line. (Robin Balmer)

'Slowly we were becoming less ignorant about control of V/STOL aircraft. We realised that in essence the P.1127 was rather like a house brick supported by a jet fountain, but possessing no natural stability or damping, and that controlling it satisfactorily with these jet reaction controls was going to extend our ingenuity to the limit.'

A.W. 'Bill' Bedford, Hawker Chief Test Pilot

Did you know?

The thrust from the Pegasus engine is directed by four jet nozzles, which are controlled by a selector lever next to the throttle in the cockpit. These nozzles swivel as one, directing the thrust from rearward to a position just forward of the vertical.

would turn the nozzles by a system of rotating shafts, bevel gears, chains and sprockets.

In September 1959, the Pegasus 1, rated at 9,000lb thrust, first ran on the bench. It should be appreciated that many V/STOL concepts had by that stage proved unflyable and that a massive question mark hung over the viability of the P.1127. Fortunately for Britain, there had been a series of American V/STOL failures, as a result of

'I felt like a bird out of a cage as I was free of the irritating, inhibiting restraints of the tethers. In the absence of radio there was a danger of going too high, with the risk of running out of fuel – hence my colleague had the red flag ready.'

'Bill' Bedford, after the first free flight

which both NASA and the USAF became seriously interested in foreign projects.

On 15 July 1960, the first P.1127 prototype (XP831) was transported by road from Kingston to Dunsfold airfield, where the final items of equipment were installed and various systems tested. The first tethered hover took place on 21 October 1960. Untethered hovering followed on 19 November and the first conventional take-off and landing were recorded on 13 March 1961. The second prototype (XP836) went straight into conventional flying trials, making its maiden flight on 7 July 1961. The initial flight trials with the prototypes showed promise, although they were short of thrust, directional stability and reaction control power in V/STOL.

A variety of modifications were applied to the six P.1127s built. The final development aircraft (XP984) had a 15,500lb static

XP836, the second P.1127, first flew on 7 July 1961 and was used for conventional flight trials, while XP831 (behind) continued preparations for transition.

Did you know?

In the early 1960s, senior officers in the RAF had the official view that 'if it did not have swept wings and reach a supersonic speed in level flight, it was not worth bothering about'.

thrust (st) Pegasus 5 and this aircraft served as a trials installation for some features of the nine Kestrel evaluation aircraft (XS688–696) that followed. The Kestrel had an uprated new swept wing, a drooped tailplane and a 9in extension to the rear fuselage. Although it had no armament provisions, it did have two hard points under the wings.

The first Kestrel had its maiden flight on 7 March 1964, and the last took to the air

The relatively cramped cockpit of the first P.1127.

➤➤
XP984 was the last of the six P.1127s to be built and became the Kestrel development aircraft. It is now preserved in the RAF Museum.

Did you know?

In the early days, the P.1127 could only have enough fuel on board for a few minutes' flight after a vertical take-off. Today's descendant, the Harrier GR9, is capable of lifting and delivering to a target bomb loads almost as great as the weight of the old prototype itself.

This, the first Kestrel FGA1, was flown on 7 March 1964.

'The Kestrel was a popular, pilot's aeroplane and the trials proved to be an outstanding success. They gave the first indications of the advantages, particularly where dispersed site operations were concerned.'

'Bill' Bedford

Did you know?

The Kestrel was never planned as a definitive RAF aircraft for possible large-scale, long-term use, but as a vehicle with which the three participating nations could experiment with jet V/STOL.

on 5 March 1965. A tripartite squadron, funded by Britain, West Germany and the USA, undertook evaluation of the Kestrels at RAF West Raynham, from 1 May to 30 November 1965. After the trials had been successfully completed, Britain retained two of the Kestrels (XS693 and 695), while Germany sold its three examples to America, where six were used by NASA at Edwards AFB under the designation XV-6A for a variety of V/STOL research projects.

Britain retained two Kestrel FGA1s after the trials had been completed. One was XS693, seen here, which later crashed near Stonehenge on 21 September 1967.

The Kestrel trials gave an encouraging early assessment of the practicality of V/STOL combat aircraft. Continuing the progress, the designation P.1127(RAF) was introduced to indicate a new line of development from the Kestrel, though sharing common ancestry. Considering that the P.1127(RAF) was claimed to represent a 90 per cent redesign of the Kestrel, the aircraft were produced remarkably quickly.

The first (XV276) flew on 3 August 1966, and the last (XV281) on 14 July 1967, by which time the aircraft had been renamed 'Harrier'.

The powerplant for these six machines and early production Harrier GR1s was the 19,000lb thrust Pegasus 6 or Mk 101. The wing itself was further developed, not only to accommodate higher weights, but also to cure the Kestrel's poor longitudinal

➤

Developed from the Kestrel, the P.1127(RAF) had been named 'Harrier' by the time the last aircraft was flown on 3 August 1966.

stability when carrying underwing stores. A more conventional ventral airbrake was also added, and, for the first time, pilots had the benefit of a 'zero-zero' (i.e. ground level with no forward speed) Martin-Baker Mk 9 ejection seat.

The Harrier's primary role in service was seen to be attacking the enemy's second-echelon armoured units in the face of relatively advanced air defences. It would therefore operate at high subsonic speed and mainly at low level, although its Hunting BL755 cluster weapons and 68mm SNEB rockets required more height in the attack phase. At that time the Harrier was a world leader in terms of its navigation/attack system, as a result of Britain's development effort on similar equipment for the ill-fated BAC TSR2. A HUD (head-up display) allowed the pilot to fly safely at high

Did you know?

Harrier V/STOL pilots say, 'It is safer to stop and land than land and stop.'

XV279, one of the two Harriers used for the development of the head-up display and FE 541 inertial system.

'From hidden sites, the Harrier Force operates using short take-off launches for increased fuel/weapons payload for the sortie – and vertical landing to reduce taxiing and 'push-back' time on return.'

Gp Capt Richard Johns

speed and low level, since it largely eliminated the need to look down into the cockpit. Its moving-map display proved an attractive feature to the US Marine Corps when they came to evaluate the Harrier in 1968.

The original plan was to have one squadron of Harrier GR1s in Britain and one in West Germany, on which basis an initial order was placed for sixty aircraft. The first production contract for the GR1 was signed in early 1967, and XV738 made its maiden flight on 28 December of that year. Subsequently the RAF decided to increase its Harrier force to four squadrons (three of which were to be based in Germany) and additional orders were approved. The single-seat Harrier GR1/1A/3 production eventually totalled 118 aircraft, excluding the six development machines.

Did you know?

Many senior officers said the V/STOL concept had too many penalties compared with conventional military jets. 'The Harrier is a splendid aircraft,' they said, 'the crowds love it and everybody applauds. But it will never be any good in a fight!' They were wrong.

Training RAF pilot-instructors on the Harrier began at Dunsfold in January 1969, and on 1 April the Harrier Conversion Unit (HCU) was formed at RAF Wittering. This is the date normally quoted for the Harrier's entry into service. On 1 October 1970, the HCU became No. 233 Operational Conversion Unit (OCU) to provide, within No. 1 Group, conversion and operational training for Harrier pilots.

'The men from the Ministry came down and said: "You must stop making the P.1154, but you can take some of the nav/attack systems out of the 1154 and try and fit it in the 1127, with an uprated engine. Then we might buy it for the RAF."'

John Fozard, marketing director,
Kingston-Brough Division

The first production GR1 (XV738) made its maiden flight on 28 December 1967. It was subsequently used as the Pegasus 10 engine test bed for the GR1A.

Harrier GR1 of No. 1 (F) Squadron, the world's first operational V/STOL unit, which formed at RAF Wittering on 1 October 1969.

In Germany, No. 4 Squadron was the first to receive the Harrier GR1, at RAF Wildenrath.

No. 1 (F) Squadron was the world's first operational V/STOL combat unit when it formed at RAF Wittering on 1 October 1969. The second to form was No. 4 Squadron in March 1970, moving to RAF Wildenrath, West Germany, three months later. Subsequently Nos 3 and 20 Squadrons also became operational with Harriers in Germany.

No. 1 Squadron continued with training for its wartime operations, making its first overseas deployment to RAF Akrotiri in Cyprus in March 1970 and to Bardufoss in Norway the following September. The first carrier deployment was made when two Harriers were flown to HMS *Ark Royal* in May 1971.

RAF Germany's Harrier Wing was tasked with providing battlefield air interdiction, close air support and tactical reconnaissance for the 1st British Corps, although

Did you know?

The Harrier was demonstrably the first truly common multi-service weapons system. It was capable of meeting the tactical needs and requirements of military services afloat and ashore.

NATO plans also allowed them to support the German Army on the northern flank, or the Belgians to the south, depending on the location of an expected Warsaw Pact thrust.

The Harrier squadrons began the development of a 'dispersed' concept that would allow them – given only the shortest of warnings – to survive any level of air attack on their peacetime base. The broad plan was that the thirty-six Harriers would be dispersed to six preselected sites, supported by 400 ground vehicles and 440 servicing and maintenance personnel, and protected by detachments of the RAF Regiment. Operating over a relatively short radius of action, the Wing was able to maintain a wartime daily rate of approximately 200 sorties over several days. Sometimes straight sections of road in wooded areas were temporarily closed to traffic for use by the Harriers.

By the mid-1970s the RAF Harrier force had worked up to an effective standard, maintaining a two-year lead over its conventional counterpart, the Jaguar. A crisis in Belize, formerly British Honduras, provided the opportunity for the Harrier's first operational 'out-of-area' deployment. Responding to the threat that Belize might be invaded by Guatemala, on 5 November 1975 six Harriers of No. 1 Squadron were flown to Belize City Airport. This became a semi-permanent detachment (as No. 1417 Flight) until July 1993. Occasional deployment exercises were continued to remind Guatemala that Belize could be reinforced very quickly.

The Harrier itself was being progressively improved. Introduced in 1971, the Pegasus

Harrier GRIs of No. 20 Squadron on the flight line at RAF Wildenrath in 1973.

► Harrier GR1 XV788, of No. 1 (F) Squadron, flying from RAF Akrotiri, Cyprus, during an armament practice camp in the early 1970s.

►► To clear the type for carrier operations, an RAF Harrier of No. 1 (F) Squadron flew trials on HMS Ark Royal in 1971.

During the Cold War period in the 1970s and 1980s, the RAF Harriers operated off base from sites hidden along the fringes of the forests of West Germany, ready to launch against an enemy as a reconnaissance/attack force, returning to cover to prepare for the next sortie. Its ability to take off and land independently of fixed runways made the Harrier a force-multiplier to be reckoned with.

A No. 4 Squadron Harrier GR3 preparing to take off from a dispersed site road in West Germany.

'The name of the game is to get off base, to seek protection through dispersal and concealment. Only the Harrier can be deployed in such a manner, operating from dispersed and remote locations, requiring very little support and take-off run.'

Gp Capt Richard Johns

powered by the 21,500lb st Pegasus 11 or Mk 103. This had a rebladed low-pressure compressor to increase mass flow, an improved combustion chamber, increased cooling for the high-pressure turbine, and a fuel system that allowed manual reversion in an emergency.

The GR3 was distinguished externally from the GR1/1A by its 'thimble' nose housing a Ferranti Laser Ranger and Marked-Target Seeker (LRMTS). This permitted more accurate ground attacks and allowed battlefront targets designated by friendly troops or helicopters to be more easily detected. The GR3 also introduced improved sensors, including the ARI.18223 radar warning receiver, with its distinctive aerial on the fin leading edge. Most of the surviving GR1As were converted to GR3 standard.

10 or Mk 102 of 20,500lb st became standard for the upgraded GR1A, together with various engineering modifications. With a noticeable change in its appearance, the Harrier GR3 that appeared in 1976 was

Wearing No. 1417 Flight markings, GR3 XZ996 is shown here flying over Belize.

Did you know?

The Harrier has a unique and legendary ability, being able to make extremely tight turns by utilising its nozzles. In air-to-air combat, these nozzles can be deployed to decelerate the aircraft so quickly that no conventional aircraft can stay with it.

The GR3 was distinguished from the GR1A by its 'thimble' nose, which housed a Laser Ranger and Marked-Target Seeker provision. (Daniel J. March)

Did you know?

In forward flight, the Harrier is at an advantage compared with conventional fixed-wing aircraft in that, in the event of stalling, recovery is possible by quickly adjusting the thrust vector controlling the nozzles, and the throttle.

'It was no new experience for the RAF to lead the world in advanced equipment and operational thinking. This time the forward stride was one of the biggest ever taken by any air force in the world. With V/STOL, the planners have given the RAF the ability to make available to local commanders in one stroke, practical and advanced close-support in the fullest meaning of the term.'

AVM B.P.T. Horsley, CBE, MVO, AFC, Assistant Chief of the Air Staff (Operational)

Through the early years of P.1127, Kestrel and Harrier development flying there was no possibility of a two-seat version being produced as, apart from other considerations, the thrust being delivered from the Pegasus engine at that time was clearly insufficient to cater for the increased weight. Looking to the immediate future and the entry into service of the Harrier GR1, it was becoming very clear that a trainer was essential.

A specification was prepared by the Air Staff for a two-seat Harrier and a contract was signed for two prototypes in 1966. It was to be a two-seat version of the Harrier GR1, to provide both pilot conversion and operational training. The aircraft had to incorporate the same navigation and weapon-aiming system, with head-up displays in both cockpits, as in the single-seater.

The front cockpit was to be as close as possible to the GR1's layout and the rear position equipped to give the instructor full authority on the flying and engine controls.

The Harrier T2 shows its bigger fuselage, flying alongside a GR1 in September 1972.

It had to fulfil the same operational envelope as the GR1 in terms of handling and strength, and eventually be cleared to carry and release external stores. It had also to be capable of being flown operationally in squadron service from the front seat under combat conditions. Much design effort and expertise ensured good vision from both cockpits, together with the safety features essential with large hood structures.

The first flight of the Harrier T2 XW174 was on 24 April 1969 at Dunsfold. The second prototype T2 (XW175) had a taller fin to improve directional stability when

XW175, the second Harrier T2, featured an extended fin to improve directional stability at high angles of attack. (Phil Boyden)

The VAAC Harrier (Vectored Thrust Advanced Aircraft Flight Control) T4, XW175, is operated by DPA/AFD/Qinetiq at Boscombe Down.

climbing steeply. Two more development aircraft joined the fleet – XW264 in October 1969 and XW265 in February 1970. Deliveries followed to the Harrier Conversion Unit at RAF Wittering and initial release to the service was obtained in midsummer 1970. When the Harrier Conversion Unit became No. 233 Operational Conversion Unit the T2 came into its own for all forms of operational flying, including weapon aiming and release.

A total of twelve T2s had been ordered in 1967, followed by a further five at a later stage. Engine thrust continued to increase through the Pegasus 102 in 1973 (Harrier T2A), followed by the Pegasus 103 in 1976 (Harrier T4). Each operational squadron was equipped with its own two-seater.

Two early two-seaters, G-VTOL and XW175, had special tasks. Hawker Siddeley, as the company was now named, decided to build its own industry-funded two-seat demonstrator. First flown on 16 September 1971 under its appropriate civil registration G-VTOL, it took part in numerous outstanding demonstrations and overseas tours, land-based and carrier-based, often in extreme conditions.

In 1983, XW175 was modified by the College of Aeronautics at Cranfield as a research vehicle for advanced control systems. Designated the VAAC Harrier (Vectored Thrust Advanced Aircraft Flight Control), it was allocated to the Flight Systems Squadron at RAE Bedford, serving for many years. It was further modified at Cranfield, and in 1996 moved to Boscombe Down.

This Qinetiq-modified Harrier, featuring modified flight controls, is currently involved in UK flight-test activities in support of the F-35B Lightning II short take-off and vertical landing (STOVL) version of Lockheed Martin's Joint Strike Fighter (JSF), which is being developed for the US Marine Corps and the UK. A series of trials started in 1999, but increased activity followed at the Joint UK MOD/Qinetiq Aircraft Test and Evaluation Centre at Boscombe Down in June 2006 and will continue into 2007. It is expected to remain in operational use until mid-2008.

Versions of the two-seater were later built or converted for the Royal Navy (Harrier T4N and T8), the US Marine Corps (TAV-8) and other overseas customers.

◄◄
Company Mk 52 two-seat demonstrator G-VTOL in its original colourful paint scheme.

In 1969 RAF Harriers took part in a transatlantic air race, sponsored by the *Daily Mail*, to mark the fiftieth anniversary of Alcock and Brown's first non-stop flight across the North Atlantic, flying a Vickers Vimy in 1919. The race took place between 4 and 11 May and was divided into a number of categories, including commercial flights, private aircraft – and military jets. The principal contenders in the last category were the Royal Air Force with Harriers and the Royal Navy with F-4 Phantoms, both types then relatively new in operational service.

The aim was to achieve the fastest time from the top of the Post Office Tower in London to the top of the Empire State Building in New York. It was planned that the RAF Harriers would lift vertically from a disused coal yard at St Pancras station, with the pilot being ferried to the aircraft from the Tower by an RAF Police motorcyclist. The aircraft then roughly followed the helicopter route from central London to near Heathrow, where it climbed to meet a Victor tanker. The aerial filling station accompanied the Harrier across the Atlantic, carrying out four air-to-air refuelling operations en route. This was the first time the Harrier had used air-to-air refuelling operationally, and the probe was a fixed fitting on the left-hand intake.

Two aircraft were prepared by the RAF for the race, both early production GR1s (XV741 and XV744). The two pilots were Sqn Ldr Lecky-Thompson and Sqn Ldr Graham Williams, both instructors from the Harrier Conversion Unit.

Prior to the race, they flew a 'recce' to find the coal yard at St Pancras, but had difficulty identifying the location of the yard and the exact route to follow. The Harriers had to fly at low level and were below the cover of any radar until they were very close to Heathrow or RAF Northolt. After a conference with the RAF air traffic controllers for the race, they bought a London road map from a local shop. This was cut up and successfully used as a 'navigation aid' during the race.

The best overall time for the London to New York leg was achieved by Lecky-Thompson, in 7 hr 6 min, with a flight time of 6 hr 11 min 57 sec. The return, eastbound flight was flown by Williams, in 5 hr 49 min 58 sec, but this was beaten by the RN Phantom with a flight time of 5 hr 11 min and an overall time of 6 hr 48 min. The only major problems encountered throughout the exercise for the Harriers was the storm of coal dust that was generated when operating from the redundant coal yard.

Sqn Ldr Tom Lecky-Thompson landing in Harrier GR1 XV744 at St Pancras railway station in May 1969.

The US Army had shown an early interest in the P.1127, and Northrop had accordingly purchased a licence, but this particular dream was ended by a new 'roles-and-missions' agreement between the Army and the USAF, allocating fixed-wing close support exclusively to the latter. The USAF had made it clear that they had no demand for an aircraft that could not reach Mach 2 (twice the speed of sound).

In 1970 the US Marine Corps (USMC) ordered twelve Harriers. The first AV-8A,

The second AV-8A for the US Marine Corps in production at Kingston.

Did you know?

The USMC's provision for Sidewinder missiles on the AV-8A led to a new dogfighting tactic. This was 'Vectoring in Forward Flight' (VIFF). The Marine pilot who performed the first evaluations on VIFF in 1970, Capt Harry Blot, fully reversed the nozzles while flying at high speed on his first test flight. He reported that he 'decelerated rapidly'. However, he could not determine just how rapidly, since he was 'curled around the stick with his nose stuck on the gunsight'.

as it was designated, was flown on 20 November 1970. By December 1976, when the last aircraft was delivered, the total had risen to 110. All were completed at Dunsfold, where they were test-flown before being dismantled and transported to

'The vision was also excellent to the front but poor to the rear; good if you are winning, bad if you are losing. The handling was superb, both for the airframe and the engine. By this I mean the stall characteristics were such that pilots would not be afraid to fly the airplane to the edge of the published envelope. The airframe went where it was pointed and the engine kept running. Who could ask for more?'

Lt Col Harry W. Blot, US Marine Corps on exploring the benefits of vectored thrust in forward flight

America in USAF transport aircraft. When it entered service in 1971, the AV-8A was powered by a Pegasus 10 Mk 802, but this was soon superseded by the Pegasus 11 Mk 803. The AV-8A somewhat surprisingly retained the 30mm Aden guns, but introduced Sidewinder wiring provision on the outer pylons, making them a permanent fit. The British radios were replaced and on delivery to the US the Martin-Baker Mk 9A ejector seat was swapped for the somewhat inferior Stencel SIIIS-3 seat.

Between 1979 and 1984 forty-seven AV-8As were converted to AV-8C standard, which offered a number of improvements. The AV-8C was withdrawn from front-line service in 1987.

Unable to purchase military aircraft directly from British manufacturers, the Spanish Government ordered six AV-8As and two TAV-8As, later augmented by five more AV-8As, via the US Navy. The single-seater for Spain was designated Harrier Mk 55 or AV-8S, and the two-seater the Mk 58 or TAV-8S. The name 'Matador' was applied to both. Entering service in 1976, this made the Spanish Navy the first in the world to operate V/STOL aircraft.

The Spanish were impressed with their Harriers and replaced them with updated Harrier IIs, selling off the surviving seven AV-8S and two TAV-8S to Thailand in 1996. These were all refurbished before delivery. The Thai Navy operated them from ground bases as well as the light carrier *Chakri Naruebet*, which was bought new from Spain. In 2006 the Thais were reported to be considering the purchase of other first-generation airframes for spares and possibly additional operational aircraft.

◄◄
An AV-8A Harrier in service with VMA-513, based at Yuma, Arizona.

An AV-8S Matador that was flown by the Spanish Navy between 1976 and 1996.

The Sea Harrier was the fixed-wing fighter the Royal Navy was not supposed to have, an interim adaptation of an old 1960s design that turned out, nevertheless, to be highly effective. Although developed for land-based operations in order to circumvent the vulnerability of fixed bases to nuclear attack, the P.1127 had touched down on HMS *Ark Royal* on 8 February 1963, less than 18 months after the first transitions had been concluded.

Numerous deck trials were successfully completed on carriers by the US Marine Corps and Spanish Navy in the early 1970s. This constantly expanding fund of experience added strong support for a dedicated naval Harrier for the Royal Navy. In fact, the RN had begun studies of a possible carrier-based variant in 1969 (the year the GR1 entered service with the RAF), but it was three years before a study contract was ordered.

The background to this contract was an MOD decision that, since the RAF would guarantee to provide air cover for RN ships by means of land-based aircraft, there was to be no replacement for carriers such as HMS *Ark Royal*. However, a new 'through-deck cruiser' was being built and the Sea Harrier itself was something of an afterthought.

In 1975 it was announced that twenty-four Sea Harriers would be purchased for the Royal Navy. The basic Harrier GR3 was given a new nose, with Blue Fox radar, a raised cockpit commanding a better view and a Pegasus Mk 104 engine to create a neat, low-cost interceptor that did not require a runway. These were comprised of three development aircraft and twenty-one

Did you know?

Like the RAF, naval aviators wanted big, powerful and very fast fighters and bombers. This unfortunately caused the full potential of the Harrier to be completely overlooked from 1965 to 1972, and even then it was another three years before the Sea Harrier was ordered.

Ship-compatibility trials began in February 1963, when Bill Bedford flew P.1127 XP831 on to HMS Ark Royal.

➤➤
XZ438, the first Sea Harrier FRS1, on the production line at Dunsfold.

➤

*The first Sea Harrier FRS1
actually to fly was
XZ450, seen here taking
off from Dunsfold.*

➤➤

*Sea Harrier FRS1 XZ451
was delivered to RNAS
Yeovilton for operation
by the Initial Flying Trials
Unit in June 1979.*

production FRS1s. In addition, the RN funded one Harrier T4A, based at Wittering, where Fleet Air Arm pilots were to be given V/STOL conversion. By 1978 a further ten FRS1s were added. In June 1982, following the Falklands campaign, fourteen more Sea Harriers were ordered, half of that number being attrition replacements. Two years later, nine further FRS1s were ordered to allow the number of aircraft in each operational squadron to be raised from five to eight. Added to this total were three two-seat Harrier T4Ns.

The 'FRS' designation indicated that the primary role of the Sea Harrier was as a fighter, followed by reconnaissance and nuclear strike. However, it is important to note that the term 'fighter' was used to indicate the interception of large, low-performance Soviet aircraft shadowing the battle group or convoy and that, in NATO exercises, Sea Harriers were routinely supported by US Navy E-2C Hawkeye airborne early warning aircraft.

In order to meet Fleet Air Arm requirements, the Harrier clearly needed a forward-looking radar capable of detecting and tracking medium-level aircraft and large ships. The radar selected was Ferranti Blue Fox. While the front fuselage was being redesigned to accommodate the radar antenna, the floor of the cockpit was raised by 10in to provide, for the first time, some rear view over the 'elephant's ears' engine intakes, as well as more equipment space.

Six two-seat Harrier T60s were also purchased by the Indian Government.

One of twenty-three FRS51s purchased by the Indian Navy, the only export customer for the Sea Harrier.

The first production Sea Harrier FRS1 (XZ450), which weighed 517lb (235kg) more than the GR3, had its maiden flight on 20 August 1978. XZ451 was the first of the series to be delivered to RNAS Yeovilton on 18 June 1979. Flying training was facilitated by the loan of an RAF T4, then by the arrival of the three T4Ns, and subsequently by three T4As.

It was found that the aircraft's warload-radius could be enhanced significantly by giving the carrier deck an upward inclination at the bow. The resulting 'ski-jump' take-off gave the aircraft more time to accelerate to a speed at which height could be maintained by a combination of jet and wing lift.

The Indian Navy was the only export customer for the Sea Harrier. Initially six Sea

Harrier Mk 51s were ordered in December 1979, together with two T60s. Two further batches were ordered in 1985 and 1986, which brought the total to twenty-three Mk 51s and four T60s. Two more T60s, modified from RAF surplus T4s, were obtained in the 1990s to replace aircraft written off.

The Indian Mk 51 was based on the Sea Harrier FRS1, but had a modified radar system and Indian-specified radios and IFF. They employed the French Matra Magic AAM in place of the Sidewinder. These Mk 51s were operated from the carrier *Vikrant* (ex HMS *Hercules*) from 1991 until it was retired in 1996, and the *Viraat* (the former HMS *Hermes* fitted with a 12° ski-jump). They were flown by No. 300 'White Tigers' Squadron. The Indian Navy explored the possible purchase of eight former RN Sea Harrier FA2s in 2006. The aircraft were available after being retired by the Royal Navy following the rationalisation of the Harrier force onto the Harrier GR7/7A and GR9/9A. Indian Navy pilots and defence representatives inspected and assessed the aircraft but it was decided not to proceed as the FA2s needed a substantial upgrade to their avionics and to be fitted with a weapons system. The Navy had stripped out these systems before the Sea Harriers were stored.

By the end of 2007, all twenty-two surviving Indian Navy FRS51s will have completed a Hindustan Aeronautic upgrade, which equips them with Elta's EL/M-2032 fire-control radar and Rafael's Derby beyond-visual-range air-to-air missile. Present plans are for the aircraft to remain in service until 2020.

The Royal Navy's introduction of the Sea Harrier came more than ten years after the RAF started operating the Harrier GR1. On 1 April 1980, 800 Naval Air Squadron (NAS) formed at RNAS Yeovilton, Somerset, followed by 801 NAS on 26 February 1981. After the commissioning of the brand-new 'through-deck cruiser' HMS *Invincible*, 800 NAS embarked for its first major deployment in September 1980. Also deployed was 801 NAS on the ageing conventional aircraft carrier HMS *Hermes*.

When Argentine forces invaded the Falklands on 2 April 1982, some Sea Harriers were still lacking their Blue Fox radars, and none of them had clearance to carry BAe Sea Eagle anti-ship missiles. However, the Sea Harrier was operational, albeit with somewhat limited capabilities, in the nick of time for the Falklands conflict.

Britain's Task Force that was hastily sent to the South Atlantic could not have been as effective without it and the outcome might have been very different.

At the same time, despite its relative maturity, the RAF's Harrier GR3 was only cleared to fire its 30mm Aden cannon and drop 1,000lb (454kg) bombs and BL-755 cluster weapons. It did not have clearance for the new third-generation AIM-9L Sidewinder (which had been supplied in haste

> *'Without the Sea Harrier there would have been no Task Force. Operating from carriers proved the concept of V/STOL air operations in independent amphibious operations.'*
>
> The First Sea Lord, Adm Sir Henry Leach,
> on the pivotal role in the Falklands conflict

➤
Preparing for another day of intensive activity on HMS Hermes *in the South Atlantic as dawn breaks on 20 April 1982.*

➤➤
A Sea Harrier FRS1 launching from HMS Invincible's *ski-jump for an air defence mission off the Falklands.*

by the Americans), laser-guided bombs, or Shrike anti-radiation missiles. Nevertheless, in order to provide more air power, No. 1 Squadron flew fourteen Harrier GR3s non-stop (some 4,000 miles) from the UK to Ascension Island in the South Atlantic. The Harriers made the trip in nine hours, refueling in mid-air five times.

The Task Force had 28 Sea Harriers and 14 RAF Harrier GR3s, together with 175 helicopters. The air war began on 1 May, when an early bombing raid on Port

The Sea Harrier FRS1 had an incredibly high serviceability record during the Falklands conflict – over 95 per cent daily, and only 1 per cent of planned missions were cancelled because of unserviceability. This was achieved by a small group of overworked aircraft, operating from just two carriers.

➤

Additional RN Sea Harriers and RAF Harrier GR3s, embarked on the ill-fated Atlantic Conveyor *off Ascension on 6 May 1982, while en route for the Falklands.*

Stanley airfield by an RAF Vulcan bomber flying from Ascension Island was followed by a dawn attack by twelve Sea Harriers operating from HMS *Hermes*. The Sea Harriers generally operated in the air combat role, while the GR3s focused on ground attack. The Sea Harriers took a toll of incoming Argentinian aircraft that was quite remarkable in the circumstances.

Sea Harriers and Harrier GR3s operated from RN aircraft carriers, which remained a considerable distance offshore to stay out of range of Argentine aircraft armed with Exocet anti-shipping missiles. This meant that the Harriers were not immediately available to support ground troops and could only spend a limited time over the islands. As soon as the British Invasion Force at San Carlos had moved inland a forward operating base (FOB) was built by the

A tragedy was narrowly averted on HMS Hermes on 21 May 1982, when a fully armed RAF Harrier GR3 XZ997 landed too close to the edge of the flight deck on return from an abortive mission. Fortunately it sustained no serious damage and was quickly hoisted back on to the deck.

Royal Engineers at a site north-west of Port San Carlos settlement. The FOB was constructed of aluminium decking, but was only half the size that had been planned because much of the material had sunk with the *Atlantic Conveyor*. The landing strip was narrow and 850ft long with a turning loop at one end, and could cope with only four aircraft. First used by a Sea Harrier on 5 June 1982, it was subsequently used by the RAF and RN as required, aircraft and pilots remaining overnight on occasions. It was known as RAF Port San Carlos to the RAF, or HMS *Sheathbill* to the RN, but was more usually referred to as 'Sid's Strip' after the commanding officer, Sqn Ldr 'Sid' Morris.

The RAF's Harrier GR3s played an invaluable role in taking over much of the highly dangerous ground/surface attack mission,

800 NAS Sea Harrier landing back on HMS Hermes *after an air defence patrol.*

Did you know?

During the latter stages of the Falklands campaign, RAF Harrier GR3s were tasked with attacking targets in the vicinity of Port Stanley using 1,000lb Paveway laser-guided bombs. It was the first operational example of this type of attack and proved to be successful.

and made 125 operational sorties. Although no Sea Harriers were destroyed in air combat, there were other operational losses. The conflict was short, and it revealed some shortcomings in both Harrier variants. On the other hand, it demonstrated beyond any doubt the unique operational versatility of the family. Without the foresight of the naval planners who had stubbornly fought for the Sea Harrier, the Falklands might well have been given up to Argentina without a fight.

After hostilities ceased, a Harrier Detachment (HarDet) of six GR3s, together with two Sea Harriers, was established at Port Stanley, becoming No. 1453 Flight in August 1983. The Harriers and Sea Harriers returned to the UK once Mount Pleasant airfield was opened on 12 May 1985 and RAF Phantoms took over the role.

➤

RAF Harrier GR3s on the aluminium planking at 'Sid's Strip', a forward operating base at Port San Carlos.

◄
Armed Harrier GR3s of No. 1 Squadron, with Sea Harriers further aft, on board HMS Hermes *in the closing stages of the conflict.*

This first YAV-8B was
converted from an
AV-8A. Here, it makes
its maiden flight on
9 November 1978.

Although the US Marine Corps was quick to recognise the potential of the V/STOL Harrier and eventually obtained more than 100 AV-8As, it was less than happy with the limited weapons payload and poor range and endurance of its Harriers. The USMC soon began pushing for a more capable version. This development was at first intended to be a joint venture between Hawker Siddeley Aviation (HSA) and McDonnell Douglas, but for various reasons both political and financial, the companies decided to go ahead independently.

The McDonnell Douglas AV-8B was designed with a new, bigger, composite-construction supercritical wing, incorporating advanced aerodynamic devices to give enhanced lift capabilities over the AV-8A. It also had a fully revised and raised cockpit.

Its new wing enabled higher take-off weights and additional ordnance to be carried, but despite a more powerful Pegasus engine the AV-8B Harrier II was about 50mph (80km/h) slower than its predecessor. With a FLIR (forward-looking infrared)

The second full-scale development (FSD) AV-8Bs featured the new wing with leading-edge root extensions (LERX), extra pylons and under-fuselage gun pods.

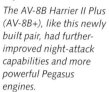

The AV-8B Harrier II Plus (AV-8B+), like this newly built pair, had further-improved night-attack capabilities and more powerful Pegasus engines.

An AV-8B of VMA-542 Tigers dropping a pair of Snake Eye parachute-retarded bombs over an exercise range.

A VMA-311 Tomcats AV-8B flying near to the burning Kuwaiti oilfields during Operation Desert Storm.

new head-up and head-down displays, a colour moving map and the Hughes AN/APG-65 radar that enabled radar-guided air-to-air missiles to be fired, this second-generation Harrier proved to be very much more capable than the AV-8A.

The early experimental YAV-8Bs were converted from AV-8As and trials began in November 1978. It was some five years later that the first production AV-8B was delivered but it was not fully operational until January 1985. Delivery of the developed night-capable Harrier IIs followed in September 1989.

The ultimate version of the Harrier II, the AV-8B+ currently in service, is fitted with the same APG-65 radar system as the F/A-18 Hornet and is able to carry AIM-120 AMRAAM and AIM-7 Sparrow AAMs, which give the aircraft a considerable in-crease in anti-aircraft capabilities. It can also carry AGM-84 Harpoon anti-shipping missiles. The AV-8B Remanufacture Program converted older AV-8B day-attack aircraft to the later-production radar/night-attack configuration. The first AV-8B+ entered service in the summer of 1994, and the first remanufactured 'plus' followed in January 1996.

When it became clear that the handling characteristics of the Harrier II were significantly different from those of the AV-8A, McDonnell Douglas produced a two-seat version, the TAV-8B. The first of twenty-four TAV-8Bs for the USMC (the sixty-fourth Harrier II to be built) made its maiden flight on 21 October 1986 and entered service in July 1987.

In Operation *Desert Storm* in 1991, three AV-8B squadrons were involved and a total of eighty-six Marine Corps Harriers flew

➤

*One of the two-seat
TAV-8Bs flown by the
Italian Navy.*

➤➤

*Spanish Navy EAV-8Bs
operating from the
aircraft carrier
Príncipe de Asturias.*

3,507 missions against Iraqi targets in Kuwait and Iraq. Five Harriers were lost, four in combat – mainly because of their vulnerability to improved surface-to-air missiles.

During the Second Gulf War in 2003, the AV-8B+ saw extensive use operating from two USMC amphibious assault ships. Each carried twenty-four Harriers, about four times their normal complement of fixed-wing aircraft. Despite its unique ability, the Harrier remains subsonic and therefore slower than most fighters. The thrust-vectoring engine nozzles leave a large infrared signature for enemy missiles to lock on to, which puts the Harrier at a big disadvantage in close-quarter dogfights. AV-8Bs continue on the strength of eight USMC units.

After successfully operating the AV-8S from 1976, the Spanish Navy purchased 12 EAV-8Bs that were delivered in 1987–8, and a further twelve EAV-8B+ in 1996. The surviving early EAV-8Bs were later remanufactured to 'plus' standard. The Harrier IIs equip No. 009 Squadron at Rota and are operated from the aircraft carrier *Príncipe de Asturias*.

Another purchaser of the AV-8B+ was the Italian Navy. The Marina Militare Italiana initially ordered two TAV-8Bs to operate from the carrier *Giuseppe Garibaldi* in the late 1980s. AV-8B+ versions were ordered in the 1990s and currently fifteen AV-8B+ and two TAV-8Bs are based at Taranto/Grottaglie with the Gruppi Aerei Imbarcati.

British Aerospace started independent development of an advanced Harrier to succeed the GR3 during the late 1970s. This Harrier was referred to as the 'tin wing', because the wing was made of conventional alloy and did not incorporate much-lighter carbon fibre. By the early 1980s, the US became involved and a partnership between BAe and McDonnell Douglas allowed joint development of the aircraft. BAe abandoned its own GR5 and used the designation for a licence-built version of the McDonnell Douglas AV-8B Harrier II. It shared the Harrier name, but under the skin was a very different aircraft, built with modern materials, including carbon composites.

The GR5 was an interim aircraft that took the RAF from the first-generation Harrier GR3 to the full day/night-attack second-generation GR7/9. This transition took more than ten years and is, to some extent, still continuing today.

First flown in April 1985, the Harrier GR5 was jointly manufactured by McDonnell Douglas and British Aerospace, with the final assembly of the RAF aircraft taking place in the UK. Although it was broadly similar to the US Marine Corps's AV-8B, the GR5 differed in detail. It was powered by the Rolls-Royce Pegasus 11 (Mk 105) with a nominal thrust of 21,750lb, it had a Martin-Baker Mk 12H ejector seat and areas of the airframe were strengthened to resist bird impacts at low-level and high speed. The number of underwing pylons was increased from six to eight to allow two AIM-9L Sidewinders to be carried for self-protection. Whereas the AV-8B had a single Gatling-type gun, the GR5 had a pair

A Harrier GR5 of No. 3 Squadron at a forward operating site in Germany during 1990.

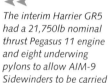

The interim Harrier GR5 had a 21,750lb nominal thrust Pegasus 11 engine and eight underwing pylons to allow AIM-9 Sidewinders to be carried for self-protection.

of the then new Aden 25 cannon. In terms of avionics and other internal equipment there were several significant replacements to keep the GR5 in line with other RAF front-line types.

Initially, sixty Harrier GR5s were ordered for the RAF in 1985, to equip the OCU and No. 1 Squadron at Wittering and Nos 3 and 4 Squadrons in Germany. A further order for thirty-four 'night-attack' Harrier GR7s

No. 1 Squadron was fully operational with the GR5 from November 1989 and regularly participated in NATO winter exercises in Norway, as here at Bardufoss in 1992. (Patrick Allen)

followed in 1988. As it happened, forty-one GR5s were built and the remaining nineteen were completed as GR5As, incorporating much of the wiring needed to upgrade the aircraft to GR7 standard. Nos 1 and 3 Squadrons became fully operational on the GR5 by April 1990, but No. 4 Squadron was equipped with the GR7 from the outset.

Externally, the GR7 could be recognised by the housing for the FLIR just forward of the windscreen.

The Harrier GR7 is basically the equivalent of the US night-attack AV-8B, incorporating very similar equipment and avionics, and has the same over-nose bump housing the GEC Sensors FLIR. Under a contract awarded to BAe in November 1989, sixty-one GR5/5As were converted to GR7 standard and were delivered to the RAF alongside the new-build aircraft. Delivery to the RAF (the Strike Attack Operational Evaluation Unit at Boscombe Down) started in August 1990 and the lengthy process of development and conversion of the three operational squadrons to the extended day/night-attack role began.

The GR7 has a night-vision goggles (NVG) compatible cockpit, which allows use of Ferranti Night Owl NVGs. From the seventy-seventh production aircraft, the

'We have to get away from the Harrier being seen as an aircraft which flies twenty minute sorties out of a wood.'

A senior Harrier pilot as the GR7 was entering squadron service in 1992

▲

Harrier pilot standing in front of a Harrier GR7, wearing Ferranti Night Owl night-vision goggles. (Jamie Hunter)

GR7 had the 100 per cent leading-edge root extension (LERX), which further delays the onset of wing rock and improves turn performance. Subsequently all of the GR7s have received the extended wing. Fitted with a TIALD (thermal-imaging airborne laser designator) pod, the GR7 can automatically launch laser-guided precision munitions. Provision of a dedicated Sidewinder air-to-air missile pylon allows adequate defence capability even when carrying a full weapons load.

RAF Harrier GR7s were successfully deployed for the first time on Operation *Bolton* monitoring the No-Fly Zone over southern Iraq, and as part of Operation *Warden*, protecting Kurdish settlements in northern Iraq following the First Gulf War. These operations required the Harriers to regain a reconnaissance capability, which

Cockpit of a No. 4 Squadron Harrier GR7, here at an off-airfield concealed site.

Did you know?

In 1993, Harriers exchanged their western European dark-green camouflage for 'air defence grey', which was judged to be more effective at higher altitudes.

Harrier GR7 showing the extended leading-edge wing root and under-fuselage TIALD pod to direct the Maverick missiles it is carrying. (Geoff Lee)

➤

*One of the RAF's thirteen
Harrier T10s flying with a
GR7 from the Harrier
OCU – No. 20 (Reserve)
Squadron at RAF
Wittering.*

had been lost when the last Harrier GR3s were withdrawn from service. In 1996, the Harrier fleet was assigned to the new NATO Rapid Reaction Force and increased in strength from twelve to sixteen aircraft (and sixteen to twenty pilots) per squadron.

In 1997 the GR7 became operational on Royal Navy carriers, delivering strike capabilities alongside the RN Sea Harrier FA2s that provided fighter defence.

In 1990 the RAF ordered thirteen Harrier T10 two-seat trainers based on the TAV-8B

airframe. It has full GR7 weapon-carrying capabilities, unlike its US counterpart, which only carries training armament. The five Harrier T4 two-seaters operated by the RN were upgraded to T8 standard in the mid-1990s.

Did you know?

The Harrier T10/T12 trainer is fully combat-capable and could, if necessary, be used in first-line service.

The RN's first two-seat T8, upgraded from a T4, was equipped with FA2 avionics.

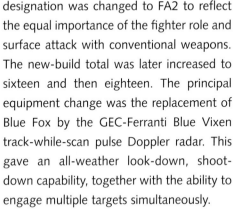

Sea Harrier FRS1s, like this specially marked 899 NAS aircraft, were converted to FRS2/FA2 standard (foreground) from October 1990.

On 7 December 1988, the MOD awarded BAe a contract to upgrade the surviving fleet of FRS1s to FRS2 standard, beginning in October 1990, together with ten new-build FRS2s. Delivery of the FRS2 began in 1994, at which time the designation was changed to FA2 to reflect the equal importance of the fighter role and surface attack with conventional weapons. The new-build total was later increased to sixteen and then eighteen. The principal equipment change was the replacement of Blue Fox by the GEC-Ferranti Blue Vixen track-while-scan pulse Doppler radar. This gave an all-weather look-down, shoot-down capability, together with the ability to engage multiple targets simultaneously.

The Pegasus Mk 104 of the FRS1 was replaced by a Mk 106, the naval version of the 21,750lb st Mk 105 used in the Harrier GR7. The cockpit was modernised, with a new HUD, two-function displays and improved HOTAS (hands-on throttle and stick) controls. It was the first European combat aircraft to be equipped with the Hughes/Raytheon AIM-120 AMRAAM.

◄
Sea Harrier FA2 ZA176 making the first successful launch of a Sidewinder AIM-9M in the UK on 11 January 1994. (via Patrick Allen)

The first operational FA2 unit to form was 801 NAS at RNAS Yeovilton on 5 October 1994. In the mid-1990s these aircraft were involved in the monitoring of shipping to enforce the arms blockade (Operation *Decisive Enhancement*), the denial of fixed-wing air activity in the Balkans as part of the international peace-keeping efforts (Operation *Deny Flight*), and missions in Sierra Leone (flying from HMS *Illustrious* in support of Operation *Pallise*). The aircraft had an improved IFF

➤
Sea Harrier FA2 of 801, the first Naval Air Squadron to be equipped with the new variant in October 1994, and the last to fly the FA2 in March 2006.

(identification friend or foe), expendable radar decoys that could be fired from the chaff/flare dispensers, a handheld Garmin 100 GPS navigation receiver mounted in the cockpit, and the latest AIM-9M Sidewinders. Five of the Navy's two-seat Harriers were upgraded to T8 standard, in line with the FA2, in 1994.

Although the RN Sea Harriers proved very effective and established an enviable reputation operating from carrier decks in all conditions, the aircraft itself became

◄

Here launching from RNAS Yeovilton's 'ski-jump' while under development, FA2 XZ439 is today the only Sea Harrier preserved in flying condition.

costly to maintain and needed comprehensive upgrades to keep it viable after 2005. A decision was reached in 2002 by the UK Government to withdraw the Sea Harrier from service and re-equip the two RN squadrons with Harrier GR7A/9s. Sea Harriers made their final flight on 28 March 2006 at RNAS Yeovilton and were stored pending disposal.

Just one Sea Harrier FA2 was in airworthy condition by the end of 2006. The experienced former US Marine Corps Harrier test pilot Art Nalls purchased Sea Harrier XZ439 in October 2005 and shipped it to Virginia. The low-hours FA2 was the second of the type to be converted and had been retained for development and trials work by BAe. Now a leading US airshow pilot, Art Nalls, together with a team of volunteer AV-8B specialists, has brought the Sea Harrier back to flying condition. He plans to have it on the US airshow circuit in 2007.

'These days we don't fight the kind of wars where our ships need defending from enemy warplanes far out at sea. Aircraft carriers are now mostly supporting shore operations by flying strike missions and it makes better sense to spend our money on Harriers, which can do that best. If necessary, we can rely on Coalition forces to provide the outer air defence for surface ships.'

Armed Forces Minister Adam Ingram on 28 February 2002, announcing that the Sea Harrier would be retired in 2006

Joint Force Harrier (JFH), established on 1 April 2000, brought RAF Harriers and RN Sea Harriers into a common command structure as part of the Joint Rapid Deployment Force. With plans well under way for the Sea Harrier to move to RAF Cottesmore to join the RAF Harriers, it was announced on 28 February 2002 that JFH was to become an all-ground-attack force. The Sea Harriers were to be retired completely in early 2006.

In 2000, Harriers operating from HMS *Illustrious* were involved in combat

No. 1 Squadron Harrier GR7 taking off from HMS Illustrious. (Patrick Allen)

With its battle tally and aggressive shark's teeth marking on its nose, one of the RAF GR7s photographed at RAF Akrotiri on its return journey to the UK after Operation Telic *in 2003.*

➤➤

A Harrier GR7A of No. 3 Squadron, with its more powerful Pegasus 107 engine. (Jamie Hunter)

The first Harrier GR9 during sea trials, with Sea Harrier FA2s of 800 NAS.

missions over Sierra Leone. The RAF Harrier force was later involved in Kosovo, and again in Iraq (Operation *Telic*) in 2003, when twenty-three RAF Harriers took part in the campaign, being shore-based in Kuwait. Maverick missiles were used successfully by a small number of Harrier GR7s involved in Operation *Telic*, although this was not a standard capability at the time. Crews from all of the RAF Harrier squadrons have been based in Afghanistan since September 2004, operating six GR7s in support of International Security Assistance Force (ISAF) from Kandahar airfield.

Improvements and modifications to the RAF's Harriers have continued. The GR7 received an upgraded Pegasus engine and became the GR7A. The capability of the GR7 had been limited by its engine, the Pegasus 105, particularly in high temperatures and during shipboard operations.

Airframe issues are being dealt with by BAE Systems in Harrier Modification Programme 3. GR7s are being modified to enable them to be fitted with the yet more powerful Pegasus 107 engine that provides 3,000lb more thrust than the 21,500lb st Mk 105 it replaces. The extra power gives the resulting GR9s improved hover, allows for extended sorties and confers better hot and high performance, as well as enhancing carrier-based operations.

The Harrier GR9 also has an Integrated Weapons Programme (IWP) enhancement, which brings together a number of discrete weapon systems, including MBDA's Brimstone anti-armour 'fire-and-forget' missiles, Raytheon's Paveway IV precision-guided bomb and IR/TV-guided versions of the Raytheon AGM-65 Maverick. The GR9 has no guns but the retained pods actually help provide additional lift on take-off and landing. TIALD pods, which provide laser designation, are being installed in place of one of the old gun blisters. Also included is the Successor Identification Friend or Foe (SIFF) system, which makes the aircraft less vulnerable in an operational environment. The work is being carried out at RAF Cottesmore, run by BAE Systems as part of the

Did you know?
During a flying display, the Harrier carries 50 gallons of demineralised water to cool the Pegasus engine, thereby enabling it to operate at a higher RPM and deliver additional thrust.

➤

First GR9 delivered by BAE Systems to No. 1 (F) Squadron at RAF Cottesmore in November 2005. (Derek Bower)

Joint Availability Support Solution project. As well as addressing airframe-life issues to extend the planned out-of-service date to beyond 2015, the programme is intended to give the Harrier a fully digital cockpit and a new open-architecture computer, GPS navigation and secure communications.

JFH received its first upgraded Harrier GR9 from BAE Systems in late 2005. It was delivered to No. 1 (F) Squadron at RAF Cottesmore as part of a £500m programme

'When I now look at all these developments I marvel at what has been achieved since I last flew a Harrier some 30 years ago. The aircraft remains unique in its capability, flexibility and versatility in "off-main-base" and carrier-borne operations. It has been proved in action and is now able to operate by day and night. The pilots have possibly the most challenging and exciting mission in military aviation.'

Duncan Simpson, Hawker test pilot

that will eventually see sixty Harrier GR7/7As upgraded to GR9/9A and eleven T10 trainers modified to T12 standard. The first T12 flew in January 2005. The improved trainers have the IWP upgrades, but not the higher-power engine.

The Harrier is due to be replaced by the Lockheed Martin F-35B Lightning II, otherwise known as the Future Joint Combat Aircraft (FJCA) or Joint Strike Fighter (JSF), between 2012 and 2015. In January 2006 the MOD stated that 'It remains our plan to operate the F-35B (Short Take-Off/Vertical Landing variant) Joint Strike Fighter aircraft from the planned future carriers. We also retain the option to deploy the Harrier GR9 initially. The design has the flexibility to be adapted to operate conventional take-off and landing if we decide to do so in the future.'

With the retirement of the Sea Harrier in March 2006, 800 Naval Air Squadron re-formed at RAF Cottesmore in April, where it was joined by 801 NAS in October 2006, both initially equipped with Harrier GR7As. Fleet Air Arm pilots had been flying with the RAF units for some time in anticipation of this move. Joint Force Harrier provided the air support for British troops as part of a NATO force in the south of Afghanistan after they moved into the troubled Kandahar province in 2005. With the personnel changing every few months, 800 NAS took over from No. 4 Squadron, RAF, in September 2006 and was soon in action for the first time with Harrier GR7As. They helped ground forces deter insurgency activity and, where necessary, attacked carefully selected Taleban targets.

The fully constituted Joint Force of two RAF and two RN Harrier squadrons at RAF Cottesmore and the Harrier Joint Operational Conversion Unit at RAF Wittering is planned to be fully operational by 1 April 2007. All four squadrons will have twelve pilots and eventually all will operate the Harrier GR9/9A and T12. The RN squadrons will continue to fulfil most of the naval tasks, but the benefit of JFH is that the two services will be operating the same aircraft type within a common structure and all will be capable of operating both on land and at sea.

In modern military planning, mobility and flexibility have become key words. The RAF Harrier Force/JFH has demonstrated these skills for the past thirty-five years. The Harrier continues to be a formidable part of the UK's air inventory and will remain so through the greater part of the next decade or until it is replaced by the F-35 Lightning II.

Did you know?

The present Rolls-Royce Pegasus, which has been at the heart of the Harrier's success, now produces two and a half times the power that was demonstrated in 1960.

P.1127/KESTREL FGA1

Engine: One Bristol Siddeley Pegasus
2/Pegasus 5 vectored-thrust turbofan

Power: 11,500/15,500lb st

Maximum speed: 715mph (1,151km/h)/
750mph (1,207km/h)

Wingspan: 24ft 4in (7.40m)/22ft 10in
(6.96m)

Length: 41ft 2in (12.53m)/42ft 6in (12.95m)

Height: 10ft 3in (3.11m)/10ft 9in (3.28m)

Armament: None

Maximum all-up weight: 15,500lb
(6,802kg)/19,000lb (8,616kg)

Number built: P.1127 – 7; P.1127(RAF) – 6;
Kestrel FGA1 – 12

Entered service: 15 October 1964

HARRIER GR1

Engine: One Rolls-Royce Pegasus 6 Mk 101
vectored-thrust turbofan

Power: 19,000lb st

Maximum speed: 737mph (1,186km/h)

Wingspan: 25ft 3in (7.69m)

Length: 45ft 8in (13.89m)

Height: 11ft 3in (3.43m)

Armament: Provision for two 30mm Aden
cannon pods under the fuselage; 1,000lb
bomb

Maximum all-up weight: 25,000lb (11,337kg)

Range: 287 miles (463km)

Entered service: 1 April 1969

HARRIER GR3

Engine: One Rolls-Royce Pegasus 11 Mk 103 vectored-thrust turbofan

Power: 21,500lb st

Maximum speed: 740mph (1,190 km/h)

Wingspan: 25ft 3in (7.69m)

Length: 46ft 10in (14.29m)

Height: 11ft 11in (3.62m)

Armament: Two detachable 30mm cannon; bombs and rockets

Maximum all-up weight: 25,200lb (11,428kg)

Range: 800 miles (1,287km)

Entered service: 1973

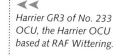

◄◄
Harrier GR3 of No. 233 OCU, the Harrier OCU based at RAF Wittering.

◄
One of sixty-one Harrier GR1s, XV758 was first flown on 6 September 1969. It was converted to a GR1A and in 1977 to a GR3.

103

HARRIER GR7/7A/9/9A

Engine: One Rolls-Royce Pegasus 105/107 vectored-thrust turbofan

Power: 21,750/24,750lb st

Maximum speed: 661mph (1,065km/h)

Wingspan: 30ft 4in (9.25m)

Length: 46ft 4in (14.12m)

Height: 11ft 8in (3.55m)

Armament: Twin 25mm Royal Ordnance Factories cannon on under-fuselage station; two AIM-9L Sidewinder AAMs; nine weapons pylons with 10,800lb (4,900kg) payload. A variety of weapons include laser and GPS-guided bombs against buildings (Paveway II and III), infrared missiles against tanks (Maverick), CRV-7 rocket pods, cluster munitions and general-purpose bombs. When required, the Harrier can also carry a pod (Joint Reconnaissance Pod) fitted with cameras to provide reconnaissance of the target and battle areas. Future attack weapons will include Brimstone anti-armour missiles and Storm Shadow cruise missiles.

Maximum all-up weight: 31,000lb (14,061kg)

Range: 2,015 miles (3,243km)

Entered service: GR7 – 20 July 1990; GR9 – November 2005

With temporary 'Arctic' paint scheme, this GR7 was en route to Norway in December 2004 for a winter exercise. (Neil Dunridge)

Fully operational Harrier GR7 of No. 4 Squadron taking off from a forward operating base.

SEA HARRIER FRS1

Engine: One Rolls-Royce Pegasus 11 Mk 104 vectored-thrust turbofan

Power: 21,500lb st

Maximum speed: 740mph (1,190km/h)

Wingspan: 25ft 3in (8m)

Length: 47ft 7in (14.48m)

Height: 12ft 2in (3.70m)

Armament: Twin detachable 30mm gun pods; four AIM-9 Sidewinders, plus two Sea Eagle or Harpoon air-to-surface missiles

Maximum all-up weight: 26,200lb (11,800kg)

Range: 460 miles (740km)

Entered service: 31 March 1980

Sea Harrier FRS1 of 801 Naval Air Squadron operating from HMS Hermes.

SEA HARRIER FA2

Engine: One Rolls-Royce Pegasus Mk 104/106 vectored-thrust turbofan

Power: 21,500lb st

Maximum speed: 734mph (1,185km/h)

Wingspan: 27ft 3in (8.31m)

Length: 46ft 3in (14.10m)

Height: 12ft 2in (3.71m)

Armament: Four AIM-120 AAMs

Maximum all-up weight: 21,700lb (9,843kg)

Range: 602 miles (970km)

Entered service: 1993

This 899 NAS Sea Harrier FA2 was painted in 'admiral's barge' markings in 2004 to mark the twenty-fifth year of the Sea Harrier.

➤➤

Registered N94422 on 21 November 2006, Art Nalls's Sea Harrier FA2 was photographed on engine tests before its first flight in the USA. This is the only airworthy FA2 in the world. (Leslie Custalov)

Harrier GR3 with a P.1127 behind – spanning the first generation of the 'jump-jet'.

PROTOTYPES & DEVELOPMENT

P.1127	6
Kestrel F(GA)1	9
Total P.1127 and Kestrel	**15**

HARRIER I

Production

Harrier pre-production	6
Harrier GR1	61
Harrier GR1A	17
plus 41 upgraded GR1s	
Harrier GR3	40
plus 61 conversions from GR1/GR1As	
USMC AV-8A (Mk 50)	102
47 updated to AV-8C standard	
Spanish Navy AV-8S (Mk 55)	11
(VA-1 Matador)	
7 sold to Thai Navy in 1997	
Total single-seat Harrier I	**237**

Two-Seat

Harrier T2 development	2
Harrier Mk 52 G-VTOL demonstrator	1
Harrier T2	10
Harrier T2A	4
plus 10 upgraded T2s	
Harrier T4	12
Harrier T4A	–
1 conversion	
Harrier T4N	3
Harrier T8	–
7 conversions from T2/T4	
USMC TAV-8A (Mk 54)	8
Spanish Navy TAV-8S (Mk 56)	2
(VAE-1 Matador)	
sold to Thai Navy in 1997	
Indian Navy Harrier T60	4
plus two upgraded T2s	
Total two-seat Harrier	**46**

Sea Harriers	
Sea Harrier development	3
Sea Harrier FRS1	54
Sea Harrier FRS2/FA2	18
plus 31 upgrades from FRS1	
Indian Navy Sea Harrier FRS51	23
Total Sea Harrier	98
Total Harrier I	**381**
HARRIER II	
Single-seat	
USMC AV-8B	235
USMC AV-8B+	27
plus 72 upgraded AV-8B	
Spanish Navy EAV-8B	12
Spanish Navy EAV-8B+	8
plus 10 upgraded EAV-8B	
Italian Navy AV-8B+	16

Harrier II development	2
Harrier GR5/5A	60
Harrier GR7/7A	34
plus 53 upgraded GR5/5As	
Harrier GR9/GR9A	–
60 upgraded from GR7/7A	
Total single-seat Harrier II	**394**
Two-seat	
USMC TAV-8B	22
Italian Navy TAV-8B+	2
Spanish Navy TAV-8B	1
Harrier T10	13
10 upgraded to T12	
Total two-seat Harrier II	**38**
Total Harrier II	**432**
Grand total Harriers	**828**

◄◄

Spanish Navy AV-8S Matador flying with a Fleet Air Arm Sea Harrier FRS1.

1957	**March:** Ralph Hooper produced the first three-view drawing of a project designated P.1127.
1957	**June:** Pressure from Hawker Aircraft led to the novel idea of a 'four-poster' thrust and lift from two pairs of nozzles gauged together.
1959	**March:** In the continued absence of official interest, Hawker Siddeley (HS) took the decision to commit funds to the manufacture of two prototype P.1127s.
1959	**April:** Bristol Aero Engines, pioneers of the Pegasus engine, merged with Armstrong Siddeley Motors to form Bristol Siddeley Engines Ltd (BSEL). BSEL became part of Rolls-Royce in 1966.
1960	**18 January:** Wind tunnel tests for the P.1127 began at Langley.
1960	**June:** The Ministry of Supply provided financial support for two P.1127s (XP831 and 836).

1960	**15 July:** Maiden flight of the first prototype P.1127, XP831.
1960	**21 October:** P.1127 XP831 made first tethered hover at Dunsfold. Its Pegasus 2 engine delivered 11,000lb thrust.
1960	**3–19 November:** XP831 made twenty-one tethered flights.
1960	**19 November:** XP831 made its first free hover.
1960	**December:** Ministry of Supply funded four additional P.1127 development aircraft.
1961	The new British Ministry of Aviation and the Federal German Government agreed to the joint development of a lightweight VTOL strike aircraft, on the basis of the P.1127.
1961	**13 March:** Bill Bedford made the first conventional take-off of P.1127 XP831.
1961	**12 September:** XP831 completed acceleration and deceleration tests and made the first full transition from forward flight to hover.

1961 **20 September:** XP831 made the first transition from hover to forward flight, and back to hover.

1961 **12 December:** XP836 reached Mach 1.2 in shallow dive, becoming the first V/STOL aircraft to fly supersonically.

1962 **10 January:** Hawker Siddeley's supersonic V/STOL design, P.1154, submitted to NATO staff in Paris.

1962 **21 May:** Under Ministry of Aviation contract FGA.236, nine further development aircraft, named Kestrel FGA1s, were ordered for a Tripartite Evaluation Squadron (TES).

1963 **8 February:** First V/STOL landing aboard HMS *Ark Royal* in Lyme Bay by Bill Bedford with XP831.

1964 **7 March:** Maiden flight of the first Kestrel FGA1, XS688, with a 15,500lb st Pegasus 5 engine.

1964 **15 October:** Nine Kestrels formed the TES at Dunsfold.

1965 **2 February:** P.1154(RAF) supersonic V/STOL programme was cancelled by the UK Government.

1965 **April:** The TES moved to RAF West Raynham and began operational evaluation.

1966 **March:** Sydney Camm died on the golf course and so, like Mitchell with his Spitfire, did not live to see the P.1127 reach maturity.

1966 Six XV-6A Kestrels were shipped to the USA for V/STOL research.

1966 **31 August:** The first P.1127(RAF), XV276, was flown by Bill Bedford.

1967 **28 December:** Duncan Simpson flew XV738, the first production Harrier GR1.

1969 **24 April:** First flight of the two-seat Harrier T2 (XW174).

1969 **May:** The Harrier Conversion Team started training RAF instructors at Dunsfold.

1969 **4–11 May:** Harriers took part in the *Daily Mail* Atlantic Air Race (top of GPO Tower in London to top of Empire State Building in New York).

1969 **1 July:** No. 1(F) Squadron at RAF Wittering replaced its Hunters with the Harrier GR1.

1970 **25 July:** The first Harrier T2 was accepted by the Harrier Conversion Unit (HCU) at RAF Wittering.

1970 **1 October:** The HCU was renamed No. 233 Operational Conversion Unit.

1970 **20 November:** The first USMC AV-8A (158384) was handed over at Dunsfold.

1971 **16 September:** First flight of Harrier Mk 52 G-VTOL (BAe two-seat demonstrator), the first two-seater with the Pegasus 102 engine.

1972 **1 January:** The Harrier Wing at RAF Wildenrath (on the German/Dutch frontier) was declared operational.

1972 **November:** Hawkers received a contract for the Sea Harrier design study and development cost plan.

1975 **15 May:** The Defence Minister suddenly announced that the Royal Navy was to acquire twenty-four Sea Harriers, to operate from three new 'through-deck cruisers'.

1976 **25 February:** First AV-8S delivered to the Spanish Navy.

1977 **5 August:** First Harrier ski-jump launch at RAE Bedford.

1978 **20 August:** First flight of XZ450, the first Sea Harrier FRS1.

1978 **13 November:** The first Sea Harrier carrier landing, on HMS *Hermes* (XZ450 flown by a BAe test pilot).

1979 **May:** Maiden flight of the first American AV-8C at St Louis, Missouri.

1979 **19 September:** The Intensive Flying Trials Unit (IFTU), 700A NAS, was commissioned at RNAS Yeovilton.

1979 **24 October:** First sea detachment for 700A NAS on board HMS *Hermes*.

1979 **December:** Indian Navy ordered six single-seat Sea Harrier FRS51s and two Harrier T60 trainers.

1980 **23 April:** 800 NAS commissioned as the first Sea Harrier operational squadron.

1981 **January:** 800 NAS embarked on HMS *Invincible* for the first time.

1981 **26 February:** First flight of the McDonnell Douglas AV-8B Harrier II at St Louis.

1981 **24 August:** Agreement announced covering the joint manufacture of AV-8B/Harrier GR5 for the USMC and RAF respectively.

1982 **13 July:** UK Government ordered an additional fourteen Sea Harrier FRS1s to replace aircraft lost during the Falklands conflict.

1983 **27 January:** First Sea Harrier FRS51 (IN601) was handed over to the Indian Navy.

1983 **21 September:** 899 NAS received its first Harrier T4N at RNAS Yeovilton.

1983 **20 December:** First Indian Sea Harrier (IN605) landed aboard INS *Vikrant* (ex-HMS *Hercules*).

1984 **16 January:** The USMC accepted the first of 328 AV-8B Harrier IIs into service.

1985 **February:** UK Government announced the Sea Harriers' Mid-Life Update (MLU) programme.

1985 **30 April:** First Harrier GR5 (DB-1), ZD318, made its maiden flight at Dunsfold.

1986 **21 October:** First USMC TAV-8B two-seat trainer made its initial flight at St Louis.

1987 **1 July:** First Harrier GR5 handed over to the RAF.

1988 **19 April:** The MOD placed an order worth £350 million for thirty-four more Harrier GR7s for the RAF, which brought the number ordered to ninety-six.

1988 **19 September:** The Sea Harrier FRS2 prototype, ZA195, made its first flight.

1988 **7 December:** The MOD placed a contract to convert the remaining fleet of Sea Harrier FRS1s to FRS2s, beginning in October 1990.

1989 **29 November:** Maiden flight of the Harrier GR7 night-attack aircraft.

1990 **28 February:** It was announced that the RAF was to receive fourteen new Harrier T10 training aircraft.

1990 **24 May:** Sea Harrier FRS2 XZ439 flew for the first time with its Blue Vixen radar switched on.

1990 **July:** First new production GR7 delivered to the MOD(PE).

1990 **12 September:** First delivery of a production Harrier GR7 to the RAF at Gütersloh, Germany.

1990 **September:** First AMRAAM weapon release trials from a Sea Harrier FRS2 successfully carried out.

1990 **September:** The first night-time FLIR trials carried out by a Harrier GR7 from A&AEE Boscombe Down.

1990 **2 October:** First ski-jump take-off by a Sea Harrier FRS2, at RNAS Yeovilton.

1990 **November:** MOD awarded BAe contract to upgrade fifty-eight Harrier GR5s to GR7s.

1991 **January:** Eighty-six USMC AV-8Bs operated in the Gulf theatre of operations during Operation *Desert Storm*, flying from Saudi Arabia and forward bases.

1991 **21 June:** The first production Sea Harrier FRS2, XZ497, made its maiden flight after conversion.

1991 **23 August:** The Italian Navy received its first Harriers, two Harrier TAV-8Bs.

1992 **2 June:** The last new-build Harrier GR7, ZG862, was delivered to the RAF.

1992 **1 September:** No. 233 OCU at RAF Wittering became No. 20 (Reserve) Squadron.

1993 **2 April:** The Royal Navy received its first Sea Harrier FRS2 (ZE695) at the Operational Evaluation Unit.

1995 **20 October:** ZH796, the first new-build Sea Harrier FA2, was handed over to the Royal Navy. The designation FRS2 had been changed to FA2.

1998 **February:** A BL755 cluster bomb dropped by a Harrier for the first time, during Exercise *Hammer Fist*, at the USMC base at Yuma, Arizona.

1998 **24 December:** Last new-build Sea Harrier FA2 (ZH813) delivered to the Royal Navy.

1999 **January:** Additional GR7s sent to the RAF detachment at Gioia del Colle in Italy to stand by for action over Kosovo.

1999 **March:** NATO raids on Yugoslavia made by No. 1 Sqadron Harrier GR7s using Paveway II 1,000lb laser-guided bombs.

1999 **April:** GR7s of No. 4 Squadron in Germany relocated to RAF Cottesmore as part of the Harrier force reorganisation.

2000 **1 April:** Joint Force Harrier (JFH) established.

2000 **June:** No. 1 Sqadron moved to RAF Cottesmore.

2000 **November:** The first upgraded Pegasus 107 engines, to improve the performance of the GR7, handed over by Rolls-Royce.

2002 **February:** MOD announced that Joint Force Harrier would move to an all-Harrier GR7/GR9 force by 2007, to maximise investment in one aircraft type.

2002 **20 September:** The first Harrier GR7A, with upgraded Pegasus 107, was flown. Thirty GR7s were fitted with the 'big engine' and became GR7As.

2003 **30 May:** First flight of the Harrier GR9 development aircraft.

2004	**January:** Newly upgraded GR7As went to sea for the first time, aboard HMS *Invincible*.
2004	**31 March:** 800 Naval Air Squadron decommissioned at RNAS Yeovilton.
2004	**24 September:** Six GR7As of No. 2 Sqadron left Cottesmore for Kandahar, Afghanistan – the first major operational test for the GR7A.
2005	**January:** The MOD launched a new aircraft support programme for its Joint Force Harrier fleet at RAF Cottesmore.
2005	**May:** The Harrier GR9's Enhanced Paveway IV integration programme began.
2005	**May:** A full-size replica of HMS *Ark Royal's* Harrier ramp was built at RAF Wittering to enable pilots to simulate deck take-offs.
2005	**May:** RAF Harrier GR7As in Afghanistan were in action for the first time against Taleban forces.
2005	**October:** Rolls-Royce ended Pegasus engine production at its Patchway, Bristol factory. The last new engine produced was a Mk 107 for the GR7A/GR9A programme.
2005	**October:** The first Harrier GR9 (ZG859) to emerge from the upgrade programme at RAF Cottesmore began flight testing.
2005	**November:** The JFH received its first upgraded Harrier GR9 from BAE Systems' Warton facility.
2006	**March:** No. 3 Squadron disbanded at RAF Cottesmore.
2006	**9 March:** The last tactical training mission was flown by the Sea Harrier FA2.
2006	**28 March:** The Sea Harrier FA2 was formally withdrawn from service at Yeovilton.
2006	**1 April:** No. 800 Squadron re-formed at RAF Cottesmore with Harrier GR7As.